A Big Mess

Written by Joe Elliot
Illustrated by Neil Sutherland, Blue-Zoo and Tony Trimmer

t-u-b, tub!

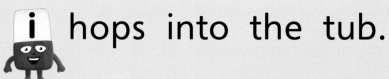 i hops into the tub.

f-i-ll, fill!

The tub fills and
fills until ...

... it spills!

Tut, tut! The tap is on!

I can not stop it!

It is a big mess!

Tip top!

o-**ff**, off!

The tap is off.